What Is the Priesthood of Believers?

Basics of the Faith

How Do We Glorify God? by John D. Hannah
How Our Children Come to Faith by Stephen Smallman
Is Jesus in the Old Testament? by Iain M. Duguid
What Are Election and Predestination? by Richard D. Phillips
What Are Spiritual Gifts? by Vern S. Poythress
What Happens after Death? by Richard D. Phillips
What Is a Reformed Church? by Stephen Smallman
What Is a True Calvinist? by Philip Graham Ryken
What Is Biblical Preaching? by Eric J. Alexander
What Is Discipleship? by Stephen Smallman
What Is Faith? by Guy M. Richard
What Is Grace? by Sean Michael Lucas
What Is Hell? by Christopher W. Morgan and Robert A. Peterson
What Is Justification by Faith Alone? by J. V. Fesko
What Is Providence? by Derek Thomas
What Is Spiritual Warfare? by Stanley D. Gale
What Is the Christian Worldview? by Philip Graham Ryken
What Is the Lord's Supper? by Richard D. Phillips
What Is the Priesthood of Believers? by Craig A. Troxel
What Is the Trinity? by David F. Wells
What Is True Conversion? by Stephen Smallman
Why Do We Baptize Infants? by Bryan Chapell
Why God Gave Us a Book by Gene Edward Veith

See all the booklets in the Basics of the Faith series at www.prpbooks.com.

What Is the Priesthood of Believers?

A. Craig Troxel

WESTMINSTER SEMINARY PRESS
PHILADELPHIA, PENNSYLVANIA

P&R PUBLISHING
P.O. BOX 817 • PHILLIPSBURG • NEW JERSEY 08865-0817

Westminster Seminary Press, LLC, a Pennsylvania Limited Liability Company, is a wholly owned subsidiary of Westminster Theological Seminary.

This work is a co-publication between P&R Publishing and Westminster Seminary Press, LLC.

Printed in the United States of America

Library of Congress Cataloging-in-Publication Data

Names: Troxel, A. Craig, 1961- author.
Title: What is the priesthood of believers? / A. Craig Troxel.
Description: Phillipsburg : P&R Publishing, 2019. | Series: Basics of the faith
Identifiers: LCCN 2019008817| ISBN 9781596389649 (pbk.) | ISBN 9781596389656 (epub) | ISBN 9781596389663 (mobi)
Subjects: LCSH: Priesthood, Universal.
Classification: LCC BT767.5 .T76 2019 | DDC 234--dc23
LC record available at https://lccn.loc.gov/2019008817

Toward the conclusion of Victor Hugo's *Les Misérables*, the hero, Jean Valjean, is lying in bed as he slowly slips into death, surrounded by his "daughter," Cosette; her husband, Marius; and a doctor. An elderly woman who has been viewing this scene through a half-closed door is so moved by the sight that she can no longer contain her religious zeal and cries out to Valjean, "Do you want a priest?" He raises his arm and points above his head, where you would have thought he saw someone, and answers, "I have one."

Christian readers immediately comprehend the religious significance of this closing vignette from Hugo's masterpiece—although from different perspectives. To a Roman Catholic it portrays a dying man's ill-advised refusal of "last rites" by a priest. To a Protestant it depicts the conviction that the priestly ministry of Christ is sufficient and needs no earthly supplement, and thus illustrates the importance of the Reformation doctrine, the "priesthood of all believers."[1]

The treasured legacy of the priesthood of all believers (also known as the "universal priesthood") has rich implications for the believer, including whether or not one needs an earthly priest at death. But all such implications hinge upon a more fundamental doctrine, the priesthood of Christ.

THE PRIESTHOOD OF CHRIST

How doth Christ execute the office of a priest?

Christ executeth the office of a priest, in his once offering up of himself a sacrifice to satisfy divine

> justice, and reconcile us to God; and in making continual intercession for us. (Westminster Shorter Catechism 25)

The Intercession of Christ at the Cross

The entirety of Christ's priestly ministry for his church can be essentially summarized as one of intercession. He intercedes first at the cross in his state of humiliation, and second he intercedes at the throne of majesty in his state of exaltation.

When Christ offered up himself on the cross for sinners, he fulfilled the priestly ministry and sacrificial system that God instituted in the Old Testament. Simply put, a priest is "one who brings men near to God, who leads them into the presence of God."[2] The priest "brought" men into God's presence because he entered the holy place as the representative of the people. This representation was symbolized by the beautiful ephod that the high priest wore with a stone attached to each shoulder piece, each engraved with six of the names of Israel's twelve tribes (Ex. 28:9). More importantly, this representation required a close identification between the priest and the people, namely, that they share the same nature. As Hebrews 5:1 states, "For every high priest chosen from among men is appointed to act on behalf of men in relation to God, to offer gifts and sacrifices for sins." This is why the human nature of Christ as priest is emphasized in the book of Hebrews. His humanity, no less than his divinity, equips him to perform his priestly ministry: "Therefore he had to be made like his brothers in every respect, so that he might become a merciful and faithful high priest in the service of God, to make propitiation for the sins of the people" (Heb. 2:17).

Preeminent among the sacrifices and feasts was the annual Day of Atonement when the high priest exercised his most sobering and privileged sacerdotal role by entering the Holy of Holies (or "Most Holy Place"). Although Christ fulfilled other sacrificial rites and ceremonies, the book of Hebrews focuses particularly upon the Day of Atonement to explain the significance of Christ's mediation.[3] On the Day of Atonement the high priest slaughtered sacrificial animals as sin offerings outside the sanctuary—a bull for him and his family, and later the first of two goats for Israel. Next he took some of the blood from each of the animals into the Holy of Holies and sprinkled the blood onto the mercy seat to atone for the sin of all the people.[4] Lastly, the high priest confessed the sins of Israel as he laid his hands on the second goat, which was released into the wilderness bearing the iniquities of Israel.

Christ fulfills this feast and other sacrifices as both the priest who ministers and as the sacrifice that is offered. First, Christ administers the sacrifice as a priest—he is the one who offered the sacrifice (Gal. 2:20; Heb. 7:27; 9:14). He was not forced to give himself, but he humbled himself and laid down his life willingly out of love for his church (John 10:18; Gal. 2:20; Eph. 5:2, 25; Phil. 2:8). He said, "I lay down my life. . . . No one takes it from me, but I lay it down of my own accord" (John 10:17–18). Second, Christ is the sacrificial victim—the unblemished Lamb who bore the curse of sin for the people that he has redeemed. In particular, it is his blood that atones for the forgiveness of sin, because "without the shedding of blood there is no forgiveness of sins" (Heb. 9:22). And it is his blood that, as propitiation, covers the offense of sin and swallows up the wrath of God.

The Intercession of Christ at the Throne of Grace

After Christ made purification for sins, he rose from the dead and ascended to the right hand of the Majesty on high. In his ascension Christ passed through the heavens and entered behind the veil (Heb. 4:14). Just like the sacrificial animals on the Day of Atonement, Christ also was sacrificed "outside the sanctuary," that is, outside heaven, which is the true sanctuary. But now in his exaltation Christ brings the blood of the sacrifice into the inner sanctuary and opens the veil of the heavenly Holy of Holies. Just as the veil of the earthly temple was torn from top to bottom when Christ was sacrificed upon the cross, so now the Most Holy Place in heaven has been opened for us as Christ has entered behind the veil. Christ has entered the sanctuary of heaven for us, bearing our nature, to obtain access for us to the throne of grace in the immediate presence of God. Through Christ then, every Christian may "have confidence to enter the holy places by the blood of Jesus, by the new and living way that he opened for us through the curtain, that is, through his flesh" (Heb. 10:19–20).

Christ appears before the Father in our nature to actively continue his priestly ministry. He sits at the right hand of the Father as our advocate and representative, constantly testifying to the verdict won by his death and resurrection (1 John 2:1). Christ can plead the church's case in the court of heaven and answer all accusations that are brought against her. And as the church prays to her great High Priest, she prays to one who sympathizes with our weaknesses, because he too was tempted but is without sin (Heb. 4:15–16). Christ appears at the right hand of Majesty fully equipped for his priestly ministry by right of his two natures of humanity and divinity, and his two states of humiliation and exaltation. As the infinite, eternal, and unchangeable God, who became flesh, Christ "is able to save [us] to the uttermost" because "he always lives to make intercession" for us (Heb. 7:25; Rom. 8:34). That is to say, his priestly intercession in heaven endures in superlative glory and excellence.[5]

THE IMPLICATIONS OF CHRIST'S PRIESTHOOD FOR THE PRIESTHOOD OF BELIEVERS

Broadly speaking there are two implications of Christ's priestly ministry for the doctrine of the priesthood of believers. One has to do with Christ as a priest; the other has to do with Christ as a sacrifice.

Christ's priestly ministry is perfection embodied. It is utterly unique, unsurpassed and unending, and never in need of supplementation or succession. It brings to an end the priestly order of Aaron, because Christ surpasses it in every way—according to the book of Hebrews, it is "better." Christ's priestly ministry guarantees a "better covenant," which is founded on "better promises" and purifies with a "better sacrifice" and blood that speaks a "better word"; and therefore we have a "better hope" and long for a "better country" with a "better possession" and a "better life."[6] In this sense his ministry is comparatively more excellent than the priesthood of the old covenant.

Moreover, Christ's priestly ministry is also superlatively excellent. In this sense Christ fulfills the ministry pictured in the unique Old Testament figure of Melchizedek, who, as a priest of God, blessed Abraham (Gen. 14:17–20; Ps. 110:4; Heb. 5:10; 6:20). Melchizedek appears without any explanation of his origin or description of his death. Scripture says that this pictures the permanent priesthood of Christ, who ministers on the basis of an "indestructible life," as one without beginning or end (Heb. 7:11–28). This is simply another way of demonstrating how both the divine and human natures of Christ equip him to save us completely—because he lives eternally and now intercedes for his church in exalted glory.

In light of the comparative and superlative excellence of Christ's priesthood, *there is no need for another priesthood*. There is a notably loud silence in the New Testament with regard to any priestly office in the gifts of offices (Eph. 4:11; 1 Cor. 12:28). The New Testament does not teach, nor even mention, any continuing earthly priesthood.[7] Those who minister the Word of God, sacraments, and discipline are referred to as "ambassadors" (2 Cor. 5:20), "stewards" (1 Cor. 4:1), "ministers" (Eph. 3:7), "servants" (1 Cor. 3:5), or "evangelists," "shepherds," and "teachers" (Eph. 4:11), but never as "priests."[8]

The second implication of Christ's priestly ministry has to do with the perfection of his sacrifice. The biblical phrase "once for all" is used to underline the superiority of Christ's priestly ministry in two ways. First, it describes how Christ does not need to minister repeatedly (for himself or others) like the priests of old (Heb. 7:27; 9:26). But second, Christ's sacrificial death is "once for all" due to the unsurpassed value of his precious blood. The priests of Israel ministered with the blood of goats and calves, but Christ ministers "by means of his own blood, thus securing an eternal redemption" (Heb. 9:12). Since it is Christ himself who is sacrificed for us, we are sanctified "once for all" (Heb. 10:10). He has thoroughly put away the condemning power of sin by the "sacrifice of himself" (Heb. 9:26). Through the perfection of his one-time sacrifice, Christ has perfected for all time those for whom he died. It follows then that *this sacrifice does not need to be supplemented*. In light of the all-sufficient sacrifice of Christ, who could demand a greater payment or punishment? Who could ask for a more pure sacrifice? Who can bring any charge against us? Who can condemn?

In the end it does not matter whether one considers the priestly ministry of Christ from the perspective of his office or from the perspective of his sacrifice; they are inextricably bound together. As John Owen stated, "The priest and the sacrifice under the New Testament are one and the same: and therefore they who make themselves priests must also make themselves Christs, or get another sacrifice of their own."[9]

THE PRIESTHOOD OF ALL BELIEVERS

The church fathers—Justin Martyr, Tertullian, Irenaeus, Origin, Clement, Chrysostom, Cyprian, and Augustine—all assumed the doctrine of the priesthood of all believers, or the "universal priesthood." Into the Middle Ages, Peter Lombard and Thomas Aquinas taught it as well. But this teaching faced increasing diminishment under Roman Catholic doctrine, which stressed that the Catholic priest was clothed with the same power as Christ and should be seen as a mediator between the believer and God. It was the Reformers who rescued the doctrine from its exile. In fact, some would suggest that Martin Luther's greatest contribution to the doctrine of the church was the priesthood of all believers. But what does the Bible teach about this doctrine?

The Sacrifice of Praise

> As you come to him, a living stone rejected by men but in the sight of God chosen and precious, you yourselves like living stones are being built up as a spiritual house, to be a holy priesthood, to offer spiritual sacrifices acceptable to God through Jesus Christ. . . . But you are a chosen race, a royal priesthood, a holy nation, a people for his own possession, that you may proclaim the excellencies of him who called you out of darkness into his marvelous light. (1 Peter 2:4–5, 9)

In one sense, when Peter sounds the royal and priestly notes of the church as a "holy nation," he actually echoes a melodic theme from the Old Testament. At Mt. Sinai God said to Israel, "If you will indeed obey my voice and keep my covenant, you shall be my treasured possession among all peoples . . . and you shall be to me a kingdom of priests and a holy nation" (Ex. 19:5–6). Revelation also picks up on this theme, describing the church as "a kingdom and priests to our God," along with its description of the priestly dress of its martyrs, whose robes—not unlike the Levites'—are dipped in blood (Rev. 1:6; 5:10; 7:14). But Peter specifically emphasizes what all Christians enjoy now.

Every Christian has direct access to the Father by the Spirit through Jesus Christ because Christ our exalted High Priest has opened the way to the Holy of Holies (Eph. 2:18; Heb. 10:19–20). Since each believer is able to approach or draw near to God in the heavenly sanctuary, the church is rightly considered a holy nation of priests. "All Christians are priests alike."[10] Martin Luther believed that 1 Peter 2:9 clearly taught that all Christians are priests, and in his usual flair added, "What man is so dumb he does not see that these words are addressed to all people in common?"[11] In the Old Testament order it was the Levites and the line of Aaron that drew near or "approached" the mercy seat (Lev. 9:7). But now every believer is able to draw near and approach God through the church's High Priest, Jesus Christ.

> Let us then with confidence draw near to the throne of grace, that we may receive mercy and find grace to help in time of need. (Heb. 4:16)

> (For the law made nothing perfect); but on the other hand, a better hope is introduced, through which we draw near to God. (Heb. 7:19)

> Consequently, he is able to save to the uttermost those who draw near to God through him, since he always lives to make intercession for them. (Heb. 7:25)

> Let us draw near with a true heart in full assurance of faith, with our hearts sprinkled clean from an

> evil conscience and our bodies washed with pure water. (Heb. 10:22)

> And without faith it is impossible to please him, for whoever would draw near to God must believe that he exists and that he rewards those who seek him. (Heb. 11:6)

> Draw near to God, and he will draw near to you. Cleanse your hands, you sinners, and purify your hearts, you double-minded. (James 4:8)

This privilege must be embraced by faith. As Christians we must believe that we can approach our Father without fear of condemnation or rejection. We must believe that we can enter into God's presence with confidence and boldness, assured that we will find grace and receive mercy to help us in our hour of need. And we must approach God assured that our prayers are offered through a high priest who sympathizes with us in our weakness and in our nature because he too was tempted as we are (Heb. 4:14–16). This is the sort of priest through whom we bring our praises and petitions, our requests and repentance, our sorrows and our joy, because Christ doesn't simply know—he understands.

Naturally, the purpose of drawing near to God is to offer worship, particularly to proclaim the supremacy and beauty of the one who called us out of darkness and has brought us into his marvelous light (1 Peter 2:4–9). This praise that a Christian continuously brings is acceptable to God because it is offered on the basis of Christ's priestly work, just as we ourselves are made acceptable before God on the basis of Christ's atoning death and resurrection (Heb. 13:15).[12] Christ's imputed righteousness justifies, and Christ's priestly ministry satisfies. Thus the adoration that a Christian offers in Christ's name rises before God as a fragrant offering. The fruit of our lips is pleasing to God. This is the worship that the New Testament encourages us to bring and reminds us we are privileged to have through our mediator, the Lord Jesus Christ (Heb. 12:28).

Our worship is acceptable through Christ because it is sufficient in Christ. As J. B. Lightfoot stated, the kingdom of Christ "interposes no sacrificial tribe or class between God and man, by whose intervention alone God is reconciled and man forgiven. Each individual member holds personal communion with the Divine Head. To him immediately he is responsible, and from Him directly he obtains pardon and draws strength."[13] And this is true whether I am alone where my Father "sees in secret," or among God's saints where the Spirit of Christ dwells and blesses (Matt. 6:6; 18:20).

The Sacrifice of Service

> I appeal to you therefore, brothers, by the mercies of God, to present your bodies as a living sacrifice, holy and acceptable to God, which is your spiritual worship. (Rom. 12:1)

In light of God's past, present, and promised mercies, it is reasonable for a Christian to offer all that they are and have to God. Our words, gifts, bodies, and talents are to be a dedicated, consecrated, and pleasing sacrifice, whether in the church or in the world.

The church is a fellowship of believers united together in and through Christ. This union, which is expressed by way of gifts, graces, and love, has traditionally been referred to as the "communion of the saints."[14] Most Christians first become acquainted with this phrase when they confess the Apostles' Creed in public worship, saying, "I believe . . . in the communion of saints." The meaning of the "communion of the saints" has fluctuated in its interpretation throughout the ages between the communion of holy *persons* or the participation in holy *things*.[15] Is the communion of the saints about fellowship or is it sacramental?[16] Since the sixteenth century, the prevailing view, including the view of the Reformers, has understood the communion of the saints to refer to the fellowship of holy persons. Reformed confessional standards like the Augsburg Confession (1530), the *Book of Common Prayer* (1549), the Thirty-Nine Articles of Religion (1563), the Second Helvetic Confession (1566), the Belgic Confession (1561), the Heidelberg Catechism (1563), and the Westminster Confession of Faith (1646) all affirm that the church is the assembly of the saints (or "the faithful") united together in Christ.[17] To put it more precisely, because all saints are first united to Christ by his Spirit and by faith, and have fellowship with him in all his work, graces, and gifts, they are also united to one another in love and have fellowship with each other in their gifts and graces, and in both their spiritual and temporal needs (WCF 26.1).

This understanding of the communion of the saints is seen in what Scripture records about the early church in its dedication to the fellowship (Acts 2:42). They devoted themselves first to the apostles' teaching and second to their mutual communion by sharing in each other's spiritual gifts, graces, and temporal needs as well. The New Testament portrays a church that is built on Christ the cornerstone and then is increasingly "built up" as each living stone does its part (1 Peter 2:4–12; Eph. 4:16). This edification takes place as each Christian brother or sister uses his or her respective spiritual gifts to encourage and help fellow members of the church family. The church cannot grow properly or soundly unless each member does his or her part. These gifts of the Spirit were given for "the common good" (1 Cor. 12:7). Each member of the church has received a gift as "good stewards of God's varied grace," and must use his or her giftedness to "serve one another" (1 Peter 4:10). Such exhortations in the New Testament are commonly referred to as the "one another" commands, which tell us that we must love, serve, forbear, forgive, accept, comfort, greet, welcome, encourage, exhort, admonish, teach, instruct, build up, confess sin to, speak the truth to, live in peace with, be kind to, do good to, pray for, show hospitality to, and have fellowship with one another. This is how the church "builds itself up in love" (Eph. 4:16). As the church displays these spiritual graces, her attraction surpasses the ornate beauty of Aaron's robe. The beauty she exhibits as a nation of priests is that of her High Priest. And the exercise of her apportioned gifts ascend before God as fragrant offerings, pleasing and acceptable to him, because they are offered not just in Christ's name but also for his honor (Phil. 4:18).

A Christian's sacrifice of service must also manifest itself in the world. While it is true that Christ reminds his people that they are not *of* the world, it is equally true that he wants them to live *in* the world. And while it is true that Christ has called his people *out of* the world, it is also true that they are sent *to* the world (John 17:14–19). Thus, on the one hand, all Christians know that their identity and priorities are determined by who they are and what they have in Christ—not by the world. On the other hand, all Christians live in a world that radically opposes them and their calling. We are to be God's holy people whose lives are marked by godliness and the fruit of the Spirit, especially love. And yet such holiness is lived out as salt and light in the various spheres of our culture and world, in which we have our respective callings from the Lord. In other words, every Christian is called first and foremost to live unto his or her Lord with godly integrity and charity. But every Christian also has his or her unique domain of vocation in which each is to lead the life that the Lord has assigned to him (1 Cor. 7:17)—whether as a teacher, secretary, builder, carpenter, banker, real estate or insurance agent, orthodontist, minister, or homemaker. In each of these spheres Christ calls us to offer ourselves as living sacrifices by loving our neighbor as ourselves and giving the reason for the hope that lies within us, because this is our reasonable service to the Lord.

The church has and always will be tempted to distort this calling in the world—chiefly in two ways. Out of the noble desire to remain faithful to their Christian identity, some Christians have isolated themselves from the world through a life of ascetic contemplation or religious devotion, perhaps even justifying it as a more spiritual calling. This is a long-standing, twisted form of what is called the "sacred-secular distinction." There will always be a voice in the church suggesting that while many of us are pursuing lawful callings in the world, they are fulfilling a higher and more spiritual mandate—something more priestly. Martin

Luther wrote in *The Babylonian Captivity of the Church* (1520) that one reason he wanted the abolition of religious orders is that they fostered conceit and contempt for the common Christian life. Another form of this distortion is the creation of Christian subcultures in which Christians increasingly insulate themselves from their neighbors through antiseptic Christian groups, clubs, business associations, yellow pages, diet and exercise groups, and so on.

Conversely, some Christians, out of the noble desire to remain faithful to living out their calling in the world, overly identify with the world. Perhaps their career or work has completely overtaken their sense of God's call on their life. Their job may even replace God himself, as the workplace becomes their temple and work becomes their salvation or meaning of existence. Some, in the name of pursuing excellence unto the Lord, have excused unethical business practices and ambition that one could scarcely distinguish from a greedy materialist. For Christians to be salt and light, they must first be salt and light: "Our problem is not that Christians are not where they should be, but that they are not what they should be right where they are."[18] Perhaps others have painted every activity under the sun as a form of "ministry" or "preaching," because they have a distorted view of an otherwise biblical notion that all of life is spiritual.

Christians must heed God's warnings not to love the things of this age, nor to become too comfortable with its ways. As Christians we will ordinarily find ourselves in tension with a world that so hated the light that it sought to destroy the True Light, our Savior. And yet, as representatives of God's love, we seek to do good to our neighbors—whether they believe or not. We are the "good Samaritans" who will rescue and help those in need who are brought across our path. Nevertheless every Christian has an equal responsibility to live in such a way in this world that it is apparent we belong to the world to come.

PRACTICING THE PRIESTHOOD OF ALL BELIEVERS

Although the priesthood of all believers is clearly supported by Scripture and enjoys the "sanction of great antiquity" in the church's practice and faith,[19] the doctrine suffers time to time from neglect. One error is to *understate* the priesthood of all believers, by overstating the ministry of some. This may happen, for example, when ordained officers—like ministers, elders, and deacons—are exalted too highly. God exhorts us to support, respect, pray for, and submit to those in such positions as they perform their spiritual leadership (Heb. 13:17). However, they are not to be catered to as if they compose a different class of citizenship in the church. No office bearer should appeal to his office in order to silence another church member who seeks to confront him about a possible offense. No pastor may argue that he is unassailable, irreproachable, or beyond criticism due to his office. If he does, he has placed himself in a dangerous place spiritually by denying the right of a fellow believer to approach him.

All members of the church must treat those in office with respect (including fellow officers), but church members must also be treated with respect, and as equals, in their capacity as a brother or sister in Christ. The church is not a place for little kings. When there was an ordained royal among God's people, the king was strictly warned to possess and read a copy of the law in order to prevent a host of temptations peculiar to his esteemed place of leadership, so that "his heart may not be lifted up above his brothers" (Deut. 17:15–20). It is possible for a church leader to promote himself above his brothers secretly in his heart or openly in his actions. If so, he has forgotten that he is a minister, that is, a servant and a table waiter (1 Cor. 3:5). He has also forgotten that, in all things concerning our mutual communion before the Lord, the gospel makes all Christians level.

The second error is to *overstate* the priesthood of all believers, by understating the ordained ministry. An idea that was common at the time of the Reformation, which continues to linger today, was that the Reformers did not go far enough in overhauling Rome's priesthood. Some have argued that the priesthood of all believers does away with ordained ministry altogether. Yet as Martin Luther wrote, "It is true that all Christians are priests, but not all are pastors."[20] Or as he wrote in his *Retractions*: "In all my writings I never wanted more than that all Christians should be priests; yet not all should be consecrated by bishops, not all should preach, celebrate mass, and exercise the priestly office unless they have been appointed and called to do so."[21] The general privileges of all do not eclipse the special responsibilities of some. Even in the old covenant there was a twofold priesthood: the *ritual* priesthood, which was conferred only on the tribe of Levi, and the *royal* priesthood, which belonged to the *whole* nation of Israelites. The priesthood of all believers "respects our 'persons' not our function, or not them as such."[22] All saints enjoy certain rights in the universal priesthood, but this does not preclude nor eclipse the place of officers in the church. As an organic priesthood of believers, "there is neither Jew nor Greek, there is neither slave nor free, there is no male and female" in the church (Gal. 3:28). As an ordained institution, there are ministers, elders, and deacons in the church (1 Tim. 3:1–13; Titus 1:5–9).

Unquestionably, both the priesthood of all believers and the ministry of ordained officers are vital to the church's health and calling. The church's goal is not to maintain a balance between the two, but rather to encourage and engender the privileges and gifts of all members. The church needs every gift, every grace, and every member in order to grow properly. The church of Christ is a body, which is held together by every joint. The church is a family, which is strengthened when each part works properly. The church is a spiritual temple, which builds itself up in love as each member fulfills his or her responsibilities. For the church to develop into the healthy and resilient body that God wants her to be, each and every member of the church must be encouraged to discharge the stewardship of their gifts in faithfulness and in devotion to the overall ministry of the church. The prayers of the whole church, whether offered in secret, in families, or in public worship, are heard and blessed by God as he pours out his grace and Spirit in response to the church's frailty and need. The service and good works of the whole church are necessary for the ministry and ingathering of the church. It belongs to all members of the church, not just her leaders, to encourage, correct, admonish, exhort, console, edify, and mutually confess sin to one another.[23] In short, every member matters.

Some gifts are more visible than others, but that does not make them more valuable. Those that appear "weaker" may actually be more indispensable. So we honor all the parts of the body and care for the whole body as one. We suffer as one and we rejoice as one. No part of the body can say to another, "We have no need of you." Nor should any member of the body feel irrelevant to the life of the church simply because they do not have the gifts of others. If all had the same gifts, the church would lack her spiritual vision, her ability to hear, her sensitivity to false teaching, her hands ready to serve, and her feet prepared to walk. God has arranged the body so that through its many members it works as one for its own good and for his glory (1 Cor. 12:12–26). We need the priesthood of all believers.

CONCLUSION

As a member of this priesthood I also need to be reminded, again and again, of the privileges that I have before God in light of the ministry of my great High Priest, the Lord Jesus Christ. I do not need any sacrifice to supplement what Christ has won for me in his death and resurrection. I have all that I need in Christ's imputed righteousness to stand before God forgiven and accepted. I do not need any earthly priest to mediate between my heavenly Father and me. I have the privilege to draw near to him directly through Jesus Christ. And as that last rite of death approaches with all of its empty threats of power, I have no need for someone to beckon an earthly priest to my side. I have one already.

DISCUSSION QUESTIONS AND ACTIVITIES

1. At what moments are you most likely to think that Christ's death on the cross was not sufficient to deal with your sin? Why do you think some Christians have no problem believing that Christ's work on the cross has dealt with the guilt of sin without actually conquering the power of sin? Why is it important to see that this is not true?
2. Scripture encourages us to bring our cares and burdens to Christ in prayer because he "sympathizes with our weaknesses" (Heb. 4:15). Why do we, even as Christians, have a difficult time believing that Christ understands the challenges we face? What does this say about our lack of confidence in Christ's ability to empathize with us?
3. Why do you think it's important to understand that a Christian does not need any other priest but Christ? And why is it important to know that a Christian needs no other sacrifice but Christ?
4. How does it comfort you to know that you have direct access to our heavenly Father?
5. Paul states that the church grows and is built up as every member does his or her part. What gifts has Christ given to you by his Spirit that could be used for the benefit of your brothers and sisters in Christ?
6. Read the list of "one another" commands on page 17. Choose two or three commands that particularly catch your eye. Now think of two or three individuals in your church whom you could encourage in their

faith by finding a way to fulfill that command in your service to them.

7. Think of your pastor or other leaders in your church (elders, deacons, Sunday School teachers) and write down a few things that you could genuinely say to them in order to encourage them. You could also pray about those things with thanksgiving to God.

NOTES

1 Hugo has neither interpretation in mind. His protagonist is pointing to the deceased bishop, who had originally given Valjean the candlesticks in order to inspire him to goodness, and who is now presumably in heaven witnessing his death. Victor Hugo, *Les Misérables*, trans. Charles E. Wilbour (New York: Alfred A. Knopf, 1997), 1429.

2 Geerhardus Vos, *The Teaching of the Epistle to the Hebrews* (1956; repr., Phillipsburg, NJ: Presbyterian and Reformed, n.d.), 94.

3 For example, Christ also fulfills the Passover Feast (Ex. 12; 1 Cor. 5:7) and the cleansing ceremony of the red heifer (Num. 19; Heb. 9:13; 13:11).

4 The priest also carried incense and hot coals to create a cloud of incense, which covered the mercy seat and preserved the life of the high priest, since sinful man cannot look upon God's holy presence (Lev. 16:13).

5 A. Craig Troxel, " 'Cleansed Once For All': John Owen on the Glory of Gospel Worship in Hebrews," *Calvin Theological Journal* 32, no. 2 (November 1997): 468–79.

6 Heb. 7:22; 8:6; 9:23; 12:24; 7:19; 11:16; 10:34–35; 11:35.

7 In Romans 15:16 Paul merely employs priestly language to describe metaphorically the intended goal or fruit of his labor among the Gentiles to be "acceptable."

8 John Owen, *The Duty of Pastors and People Distinguished*, vol. 13 of *The Works of John Owen*, ed. William H. Goold (Edinburgh: Banner of Truth Trust, 1967), 26; Martin Luther, "Dr. Luther's Retraction of the Error Forced upon Him by the Most Highly Learned Priest

of God, Sir Jerome Emser, Vicar in Meissen," in *Luther's Works* [1521], 39.229. The Roman Catholic Church has maintained a contrary opinion: "If any one saith, that there is not in the New Testament a visible and external priesthood; or that there is not any power of consecrating and offering the true body and blood of the Lord, and of forgiving and retaining sins; but only an office and bare ministry of preaching the Gospel, or, that those who do not preach are not priests at all; let him be anathema." The Council of Trent, Session 23 (July 15, 1563), "Sacraments of Order," Canon 1.

9 Owen, *Duty*, 26.

10 J. B. Lightfoot, *St. Paul's Epistle to the Philippians* (1868; repr., Lynn, MA: Hendrickson, 1981), 185.

11 Martin Luther, *Luther's Works*, American ed., vol. 39, *Church and Ministry I*, ed. Eric W. Gritsch (Philadelphia: Fortress Press, 1970), 229, 235. Jerome Emser argued that "the salt of the earth" refers to priests. To which Luther responded: "So 'salt' means 'priests,' 'incense' means 'vicar,' 'water' means 'sacristan,' 'fire' means 'schoolmaster,' and 'straw' means 'pupils.' . . . Now I am satisfied. . . . Who can with good argument refute the fact that 'salt' means 'priest'?" Luther, *Works*, 39.233.

12 Thomas Manton, *The Works of Thomas Manton*, "Sermons on Revelation 1.5,6" (Birmingham, AL: Solid Ground Christian Books, 2008) 19.91–92.

13 Lightfoot, *Philippians*, 181. This stands in stark contrast to Roman Catholic canon law. The Council of Trent declared, "If any one affirm that all Christians indiscriminately are priests of the New Testament or that they are all mutually endowed with an equal spiritual power, he clearly does nothing but confound the ecclesiastical hierarchy, which is an army set in array." Session 23 (July 15, 1563), "Sacraments of Order," Canon 4.

14 The phrase actually first appeared in the "Old Roman Creed" (or "Shorter Roman Symbol"), the undisputed progenitor of the Apostles' Creed. The phrase was a late addition to the Creed. It did not appear before the fifth century nor in any of its treatments by Ignatius of Antioch, Justin Martyr, Irenaeus's "Rules of Faith," Tertullian, Ambrose, and Augustine; nor is it found in the creeds of Caesarea (325), Nicea (325), and Constantinople (381). John H.

Leith, ed., *Creeds of the Churches*, 3rd ed. (Atlanta: John Knox, 1982), 22; J. N. D. Kelly, *Early Christian Creeds*, 3rd ed. (New York: Longman, 1972), 127.

15 Werner Elert has said, "The history of the interpretation of *sanctorum communio* is the history of the Western interpretation of the Church." Werner Elert, *Eucharist and Church Fellowship in the First Four Centuries*, trans. N. E. Nagel (St. Louis: Concordia, 1966), 8. The two ideas have been combined in Eastern Orthodoxy's well-known phrase, *Sancta sanctis* ("Holy things for holy people").

16 The controversy arises from whether *sanctorum* (a genitive plural) refers to "holy people" (masculine genitive plural—*sancti*), or to "holy things" (neuter plural genitive—*sancta*).

17 Although these Reformed standards affirm the mystical union between those saints on earth (the church *militant*) and the saints in heaven (the church *triumphant*), they deny any veneration of, or prayers to, the saints who have died. Furthermore, they deny any notion of saints in "purgatory" (the church *expectant*).

18 Os Guinness and John Seel, eds., *No God but God: Breaking with the Idols of Our Age* (Chicago: Moody Press, 1992), 17.

19 Henry Fielding, *Joseph Andrews* (New York: Modern Library, 1950), 92.

20 Luther, *Works*, 13.65, quoted in Bernard Lohse, *Martin Luther's Theology: Its Historical and Systematic Development*, trans. and ed. Roy A. Harrisville (Minneapolis: Fortress Press, 1999), 290.

21 Luther, *Works*, 39.233.

22 Owen, *Duty*, 21

23 John R. Crawford, "Calvin and the Priesthood of All Believers," *Scottish Journal of Theology* 21 (1968): 154.

ALSO FROM P&R PUBLISHING

We might be relieved if God placed our sanctification only in the hands of trained professionals, but that is not his plan. Instead, through the ministry of every part of the body, the whole church will mature in Christ.

Paul David Tripp helps us discover where change is needed in our own lives and the lives of others. Following the example of Jesus, Tripp reveals how to get to know people, and how to lovingly speak truth to them.

"Helps us help others (and ourselves) by giving grace-centered hope that we can indeed change, and by showing us the biblical way to make change happen."

—**Skip Ryan**

"A wonderful application of the old Gaelic saying, 'God strikes straight blows with crooked sticks.' As inadequate as we are, God is eager to use us to help others change. The more you apply the biblical principles discussed in this book, the more readily you will fit into his mighty hand."

—**Ken Sande**

ALSO FROM P&R PUBLISHING

There are so many misconceptions about Calvinism that it is safe to say that even most Christians do not truly know what it teaches. You may have grown up in a Reformed church, or you may have heard about Calvinism mostly in arguments. Either way, it may surprise you to know that this belief has huge, and very *positive*, implications for a believer's daily life!

Jim Orrick clears up misinformation about Calvinism and explains its basic yet profound ideas and teachings—using the Bible as the basis for everything he says.

Making use of relatable life illustrations, as well as an engaging, clear, and friendly style, he sets out the basics of what Calvinism teaches, explores each of the five points that summarize its positions, and addresses rebuttals and misunderstandings. Learn why the teachings of Calvinism not only matter, but can renew your trust and hope in the gospel!

ALSO FROM P&R PUBLISHING

Pastor and seminary professor Sean Michael Lucas suggests that being Presbyterian means embracing distinctive beliefs, practices, and stories as one's own. As new members, church officers, and potential Presbyterians read about beliefs, practices, and stories, they will understand and move to embrace this way of being Christian. Written in a nontechnical style, *On Being Presbyterian* is a unique resource for equipping believers and introducing them to Presbyterian church practice.

"At last a brief, popular introduction to Presbyterianism that I can put in the hands of Bible-believing, gospel-loving Presbyterians and other evangelicals interested in this part of the Christian family. Readable, sympathetic, and circumspect."

—**J. Ligon Duncan III**

Was this booklet helpful to you?
Consider writing a review online.
The author appreciates your feedback!

Or write to P&R at editorial@prpbooks.com
with your comments. We'd love to hear from you.